Good-bye, Sam!

by Hadley Ruddock
illustrated by Laura Gibbons Nikiel

 HOUGHTON MIFFLIN   BOSTON

Printed in China

ISBN-13: 978-0-547-01729-7
ISBN-10: 0-547-01729-4

4 5 6 7 8 9 0940 15 14 13 12 11 10

Mama Bear said, "Can you please clean your room?"

"Yes," Sam said.
"I can clean my room."

So Sam made his bed.
He picked up his clothes and
his toys, too.

"Good job, Sam!"
said Mama Bear.
"Thanks," Sam said.
"Now I can read my book."

Then Papa Bear said,
"Can you please play
with the baby?"

"Yes," Sam said.
"I can play with the baby."

So Sam played with the baby.
He made funny faces and
silly sounds.
He played with all her toys.

Papa Bear said,
"Good job, Sam!"
"Thanks," said Sam.
"Now I can read my book."

But did Sam read
his book?
Not now!

Responding

✔ TARGET SKILL **Story Structure**

Where does this story take place? Who are the characters? Tell what happens in the story. Make a chart.

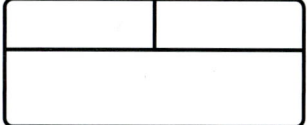

✏ Write About It

Text to World Draw a picture of Sam. Label your picture. Then make a list of the things he does in the story.

WORDS TO KNOW

good | **said**

LEARN MORE WORDS

faces | **sounds**

TARGET SKILL **Story Structure**

Tell the setting, characters, and events in a story.

TARGET STRATEGY **Analyze/Evaluate**

Tell how you feel about the text, and why.

GENRE **Fiction** is a story that is made up.